EXCEL
IF FUNCTION
CHAMPION

HENRY E. MEJIA

EXCEL IF FUNCTION CHAMPION

Copyright © 2020 HENRY E. MEJIA

DEDICATION

To my parents, who have taught me that life is about
overcoming obstacles and enjoying it.

CONTENTS

ACKNOWLEDGMENTS

I would like to thank all those who supported me throughout the creation of this book, either with words of encouragement or with ideas to improve it

INTRODUCTION

Welcome to Excel IF Function Champion. This book was written to teach you the correct way to use the IF Functions and other logical functions quickly and easily.

It is extremely important that you know that this book is not just about the IF function, it is actually a complete guide about the main logical functions of Excel, so with this book you will also learn to use the following Excel Functions:

- IF
- IFS
- OR
- AND
- SUMIF
- SUMIFS

- COUNTIF
- COUNTIFS

This book is part of the "Excel Champions Series" and is written in a simple and clear language.

Many times, it is necessary to use reasoning to make decisions. In Excel there are the LOGICAL functions to make those decisions and then obtain a specific result.

These logical functions are what you must master to create formulas that make the reasoning process for you, saving time and effort. Additionally, Excel formulas can not be wrong if you write them correctly.

It's time to start your journey to become an Excel IF Function Champion.

.

GET YOUR 25 PRACTICE SPREADSHEETS (.XLSX)

Before starting Chapter 1 I recommend you get your 25 practice spreadsheets. Those will help you at the end of each chapter to practice what you have learned and make sure you have learned it well.

To get them immediately just **Scan this QR Code** or go directly to https://bit.ly/hemejia2 and follow the **instructions.**

If for any reason both the QR Code and the Link don't work, send an email to ems.online.empire@gmail.com saying:

"Hello, I bought your book EXCEL IF FUNCTION CHAMPION and I need the 25 practice spreadsheets".

I will gladly reply to you but you may need to wait a few business days.

Now you are ready to start Chapter 1. Let's go!

CHAPTER 1:

WHAT IS A FUNCTION AND WHICH ARE ITS BENEFITS? (CHAPTER FOR BEGINNERS)

This chapter is written as an introduction for those who have no knowledge of Excel Functions and for those who have some knowledge but find it a little confusing yet. If you already know how to use some other excel functions, you may need to skip this chapter, although it would not hurt to review it.

An Excel Function is a way to carry out some operation in Excel. They are also called FORMULAS.

EXCEL FUNCTIONS = EXCEL FORMULAS

Microsoft Excel divides the functions into groups, and the main ones are the following:

• Financial

• Logical

• Text

• Date and Time

• Lookup & Reference

• Mathematical & Trigonometric

The IF Function (and most of the formulas we will study in this book fall into the LOGICAL category)

ADVANTAGES OF FUNCTIONS

The biggest benefit of the functions is that you can save a lot of time since the Excel can automatically perform reasoning such as:

• Decide WHAT to write if a certain condition is met

• Decide WHAT to write if the condition is not met

• Decide WHAT operation to do depending on the situation

• Decide WHEN to add and when NOT

• Search for specific data

• Decide WHERE to look for this data

• Decide WHEN to look for this data

• And many other operations that you do not need to do manually if you know how to use Excel Functions

WHERE DO I FIND THE FUNCTIONS I CAN CHOOSE?

Option 1: Look for the Formulas tab and there you can find them divided into categories.

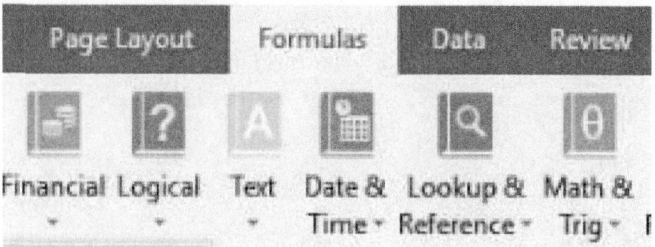

Option 2: Click on the FX button located to the left of the formula bar. And you will be shown a box with all the formulas.

Option 3: Write the formula directly in the formula bar.

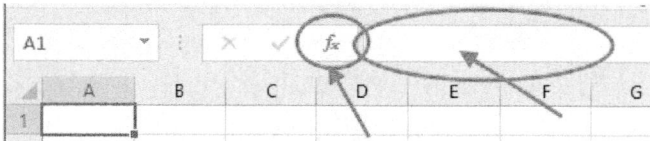

WHICH ONE IS THE BEST OPTION AND WHY?

I sincerely believe that Option 3 (write the formula) is better because with some practice you learn the Arguments (Parts) of each formula, plus it is faster to add the formulas by writing them.

WHICH ARE THE PARTS OF A FUNCTION?

The functions always start with the equals symbol (=) followed by the formula name (for example IF) followed by the parts of the formula (also known as arguments). The arguments are separated by a comma (,) in case the function has several arguments.

For example, the IF formula has 3 arguments and to use it would be written like this:

=IF(argument1,argument2,argument3)

Obviously instead of writing argument1,2 and 3 you need to use other parameters but I will explain exactly how it works in the next chapter.

At this moment my main intention is that you understand that the Excel functions always have the format of **=NAMEOFTHEFORMULA (arguments)** and without any space in the whole formula!

QUICK CHAPTER SUMMARY:

- Functions perform operations so that you do not have to waste time on them.
- The main benefit is that they save time and avoid errors
- Its structure is always **=NAME(arguments)**

CHAPTER 2:

IF FUNCTION

WHAT IS IF FUNCTION FOR?

The IF FUNCTION is used to perform logical tests and, depending on the result of this test, Excel will show one of two possible results.

If the logical test is TRUE Excel will do what you ask it to do when it is TRUE, if it is FALSE Excel will do what you ask it to do when it is FALSE.

"IF FUNCTION can return 2 different results, depending on whether the logical test turns out to be true or false."

IMPORTANT NOTE: Later we will see some variants with which you can increase the number of possible results to 3 or more.

OTHER IMPORTANT NOTE: Later we will see other variants with which you can perform 2 or more logical tests at the same time.

WHICH ARE THE PARTS OF THE IF FUNCTION?

Remember that the "parts" are called Arguments, and we are going to analyze them at this time.

In your Excel formula bar, write exactly the following:

= IF (

You can see that a box is displayed that says:

(Logical Test, Value if True, Value if False)

Those are the 3 Arguments of the IF

Function! Separated by a comma and ready to be written. But not so fast, before I have to explain to you what each argument is for.

Before continuing, the STRUCTURE or SYNTAX of the IF Function is then as follows:

=IF(Logical Test**,** Value if True**,** Value if False**)**

WHAT IS EVERY ARGUMENT FOR?

LOGICAL TEST: It is the test that Excel will perform and will determine if it is TRUE or FALSE. In this argument there are several questions (tests) that can be done, such as the following (they are general examples to make more understandable how the tests work):

• Is the number in X cell greater than the number in X cell?

• Is X cell smaller than X cell?

• Is X cell the same as X cell?

• Is the TEXT in X cell the same as the text in X cell?

• Is the text of X cell "DELIVERED"?

• Is the number in X cell greater than or equal to X number?

• Is the date in X cell after X date?

• Is the result of adding X cell and X cell greater than X number?

As you can see, there are many examples of questions (logical tests) that you can perform in Argument 1. In the exercises we will practice many of these examples.

VALUE IF TRUE: If the answer to the test made in argument 1 is TRUE, it will show what you set here in Argument 2. Some examples of response can be:

• Some specific text that you want as "YES", "NO", "APPROVED", "DELIVERED".

• Some arithmetic operation

• ANOTHER EXCEL FUNCTION! That's right, you can put a function INSIDE another function, they are called "NESTED FUNCTIONS", and we will also see how to use them in the following chapters.

Then, if the logical test is TRUE, you will obtain the text, operation or formula that you write in Argument 2.

VALUE IF FALSE: I think you already know what is going to happen with this Argument. If the logical test is FALSE, you will get Argument 3.

In the same way as Argument 2, you can use texts, arithmetic operations or other formulas.

IT IS SHOW TIME! START WITH THE EXERCISES!

Maybe you're thinking "But you haven't taught me how to use the IF Function yet!". In case you didn't know, my teaching method is through exercises. It is so much easier for you to learn if we are doing the exercise together, at the same time that I am explaining everything to you.

SUPER IMPORTANT NOTE: Every time you want to write the name of a cell in the formula (for example B4) or a full range (for example B4:B10, which means B4 to B10) you can:

1. Simply the cell clicking on it while you write the formula, in case of being a cell

2. Select the range of cells (click and drag cursor) while you write the formula, if there are several cells.

Exercise: Chapter2ex1.xlsx

When you open the exercise, you will find a list of student names and their grades. You need to use the IF Function in Column C to determine if they approved or failed.

Step 1: Position yourself in cell C4 and when double clicking you will notice that you can also write the formula directly in the cell. It is important to remember that the formula must be written in column C.

	A	B	C
3	**NAME**	**GRADE**	**STATUS**
4	Wenona Rocchio	98	
5	Conchita Benford	71	
6	Becki Davalos	43	
7	Deadra Hammersley	55	
8	Rosy Westman	30	
9	Elden Eudy	47	
10	Willian Hamlett	74	
11	Rona Arsenault	44	
12	Talisha Marcum	65	

Step 2: You need to be aware that at the time of writing the formula you will need to apply the following logical test:

B4>=60

And what the hell does that mean? In the Excel language it means "If cell B4 is

Greater than or equal to 60".

And how can you write greater than or equal to 40? **B4>=40**

And how can you write LESS or equal to 50? **B4<=50**

And how can you write B5 equal to 50? **B5=50**

Every logical test needs to be written without spaces between symbols

For this type of logical tests, you can see that the **symbols > < =** are extremely important. Let's continue with step 3, remembering that our logical test in this exercise is **B4>=60** and we could read it saying "If B4 is greater than or equal to 60 then ..."

Step 3: The complete formula that you should write in C4 would be the following:

=IF(B4>=60,"Approved","Failed")

NOTE: Remember that you can click on B4 instead of manually entering B4

What does that complicated formula mean? I will answer it in parts:

=IF is used because the symbol **=** indicates the start of a function and because **IF** is the name of the function

The open parenthesis **(** means that we will start to write the arguments of the function

B4> =60, is the first argument (the logical test) followed by a comma, which indicates the completion of the logical test

"Approved", It is the second argument (Value if TRUE). It is between quotes **" "** because it is the specific TEXT that I want Excel to write in case the logical test is True. And at the end the comma that indicates the end of the second argument.

IMPORTANT NOTE: Each time you want some specific text, you must put it between quotation marks " ".

"Failed") It is the third argument (Value if False), it is the TEXT that we want Excel to write if the logical test is False. Finish the formula by closing a parenthesis **)** and press ENTER to get the result.

To summarize the formula =IF(B4>=60,"Approved","Failed") we could read it in the following way: **"If B4 is greater than or equal to 60 then write Approved, if it is NOT greater than or equal to 60 then write Failed."**

	A	B	C
3	**NAME**	**GRADE**	**STATUS**
4	Wenona Rocchio	98	Approved

You can see that since the Grade is greater than 60, Excel wrote **Approved** for Wenona Rocchio.

Step 4: The last step is to go through the formula to use that same formula in all students. How do you do that? Simply select Cell C4 (where you wrote the formula), click on the little dot that appears in the lower right corner and drag down the formula without releasing the click.

	A	B	C
3	**NAME**	**GRADE**	**STATUS**
4	Wenona Rocchio	98	Approved

You will automatically get the result without making any other calculation. Why? Because the formula is moved automatically, that is, cell C4 performs the logical test on cell B4, but cell C5 performs the logical test on cell B5, and C6 on B6, etc.

That way you can get all the results quickly.

	A	B	C
3	**NAME**	**GRADE**	**STATUS**
4	Wenona Rocchio	98	Approved
5	Conchita Benford	71	Approved
6	Becki Davalos	43	Failed
7	Deadra Hammersley	55	Failed
8	Rosy Westman	30	Failed
9	Elden Eudy	47	Failed
10	Willian Hamlett	74	Approved
11	Rona Arsenault	44	Failed
12	Talisha Marcum	65	Approved

CONGRATULATIONS! You have created your first IF Function. It is a small step that opens the possibilities to dominate that formula in a more complex way in the following chapters.

As you can see, this logical test can help you complete a lot of important information without the need to manually type.

This was an exercise where the result is a "Specific Text", in the next chapter we will do exercises where the result is an arithmetic operation, for that we must place a small formula INSIDE an argument of the IF Function. But first, I invite you to practice with more exercises.

SIMILAR EXERCISES:

It's time for you to solve more exercises and practice. Once you complete them you can advance to the next IF Function chapter.

Chapter2ex2.xlsx

Chapter2ex3.xlsx

QUICK CHAPTER SUMMARY:

- The IF Function is used to perform a logical test and Excel provides you with 1 of 2 possible outcomes
- The logical test can be true or false
- You can also expand the number of possible outcomes to 3, 4, 5 or more

- The arguments of the IF Function can contain Text, Arithmetic Operations or even another function.
- In this chapter we performed exercises where the results were some specific text.

CHAPTER 3:

IF FUNCTION WITH ARITHMETIC OPERATIONS IN ARGUMENTS "VALUE IF TRUE" AND "VALUE IF FALSE"

Now that you know how the IF Function arguments work, we can move faster with more examples and exercises.

In this chapter you will add 2 important features to your knowledge of the IF Function:

1. You will learn to use a text logical testof

2. You will learn to use arithmetic operations in the Value if True and Value if False arguments.

EXERCISE: Chapter3ex1.xlsx

In the exercise there are 5 car salesmen, each sold a car brand today. The commission for each car seller is 3% but during the morning meeting the sales manager announced that whoever sold a BMW would get an extra 1% as a bonus per sale. The following exercise is small, however it will serve as training to solve the most complex exercises.

Step 1: Position yourself in cell E4 to start writing the IF Function.

Step 2: The logical test in this case will be the following:

A4=”BMW”

Why? The reason is that we need Excel to determine who did sell a BMW and who did not sell a BMW. In column A you can find all the sales brands, that's why we started with that logical test.

At the moment our formula in E4 starts like this:

=IF(A4="BMW",

And you could read it like this: *"If A4 is equal to" BMW "then ..."*

NOTE: Notice that the word **"BMW"** is in quotes **""**.

Correct: **=IF(A4=BMW,** without quotes you will get an error

Incorrect: **=IF(A4="BMW",**

Step 3: If the logical test is True (if it sold a BMW) we will obtain the result of Argument 2. Then argument 2 (Value If True) must be the arithmetic operation that would result in 3% commission plus 1% of the bonus for selling the BMW.

It could be: **B4*(D4+.01),**

Or it could be: **B4*(.03+.01),**

Why? **B4** is the total value of the sale, **D4** is the normal commission percentage (3%). Since the normal commission is already in the table in column D, you can use **D4** or you can write directly **.03** which means 3%. Additionally, you must add that 1% of the bonus bonus, so you write **.01**

So **B4*(D4+.01)** means that:

1. First excel adds what is inside the parentheses, which is D4+.01, which is equal to .04 (or what is the same, 4%)

2. Then Excel multiplies B4 * .04 thus obtaining the total commission amount with the bonus bonus for selling a BMW.

The formula now looks like this:
=IF(A4="BMW",B4*(D4+.01),

And you could read it like this: *"If A4 is equal to "BMW" then write the result of the multiplication of B4 TIMES the sum of D4 plus .01"*

Step 4: If the logical test is False (if the seller did not sell a BMW) we will get the result of Argument 3. Then argument 3 (Value If False) must be the arithmetic operation that would result in only 3% commission for the sale

It could be: **B4*D4**

Or it could be: **B4*.03**

Why? Because if you do not sell a BMW you only need to multiply the value of the car by 3% commission.

The **COMPLETE** formula now looks like this:

=IF(A4="BMW",B4*(D4+.01),B4*.03)

And you could read it like this: *"If A4 is equal to" BMW "then write the result of the multiplication of B4 TIMES the sum of D4 plus .01, if A4 is NOT equal to "BMW" then write the result of B4 times*

3% "

Step 5: Drag the same formula for all the names and you will get the following result.

	A	B	C	D	E
3	BRAND	SALE	SOLD BY	REGULAR COMISION	TOTAL PAYMENT
4	Benz	$ 40,000	Viki Jerabek	3%	$ 1,200
5	BMW	$ 35,000	Sana Ulery	3%	$ 1,400
6	Ford	$ 10,000	Leida Schow	3%	$ 300
7	Chevrolet	$ 12,000	Christiane Polen	3%	$ 360
8	BMW	$ 30,000	Tonja Berk	3%	$ 1,200

It is clearly observed that Sana Ulery and Tonja Berk generated more profits. If you do the maths you will see that they earned 4% on their sale, while all the others only 3%. You have achieved this thanks to your knowledge with the IF Function.

CONGRATULATIONS! Now you know how to create IF Functions with arithmetic operations in arguments 2 and 3.

In the next chapter you will learn how

to perform a logical test with arithmetic operation, so Excel will first do the arithmetic operation, then confirm if it is True or False and then return a result.

SIMILAR EXERCISES:

It's time for you to solve more exercises and practice. Once you complete them you can advance to the next IF Function chapter.

Chapter3ex2.xlsx

Chapter3ex3.xlsx

QUICK CHAPTER SUMMARY:

• You can search for Specific Text in your logical test

• You can use arithmetic operations in Value If True and Value If False arguments

Are you enjoying this book?

Do you think it's easy to understand?

Have the exercises helped you learn faster?

Without knowing your opinion I won't know if the book has helped you to become a better IF FUNCTION user.

You can share your thoughts with me by simply writing a **Review on Amazon.**

CHAPTER 4

IF FUNCTION WITH ARITHMETIC OPERATIONS AND NESTED FUNCTIONS IN THE LOGICAL TEST

In this chapter you will learn how to use arithmetic operations in the logical test, so Excel will perform the following process:

1. First, perform the arithmetic operation

2. After, Excel will determine if the logical test is True or False

3. Finally you will get the corresponding outcome.

Of course, all this is done by Excel in less than a second once you have the written formula.

Some other things of great importance that you will learn are the following:

• You will see that arithmetic operations can be performed on arguments 1, 2, and 3 at the same time.

• You will also notice that in the logical test you can combine arithmetic operations with symbols such as greater (>), less (<) or equal (=).

But the most important thing you will learn in this chapter is to use NESTED FUNCTIONS. The NESTED FUNCTIONS are functions within other functions. In other words, each argument of the IF Function will be another function. Let me exemplify it like this.

=IF(Another Function, Another Function, Another Function)

In this way you will begin to use IF in a much more advanced way. Show time! Let's start with the exercise.

EXERCISE: Chapter 4ex1.xlsx

In the exercise you have the name of 4 sellers and sales from January to March. The seller with more than $ 100,000 in accumulated sales in those 3 months will get an extra bonus of 2%, but the seller who did not achieve the goal will not get a bonus.

If the seller achieved the goal you must calculate how much money he will get as a bonus, if he did not achieve it you must show the "No Bonus" tag.

Step 1: We will create the logical test knowing the following: "If the sum of the 3 months is equal to or greater than $ 100,000 then ...". Ready, that is the logical test that we must translate.

Do you remember that you would learn to use the Nested Functions in this chapter? The time has come to do it. Position yourself in cell E4, there you must write the formula.

IF=(SUM(B4:D4)>=100000,

And what the hell does that mean? Let's explain it in parts:

IF=(SUM(B4:D4)>=100000, means that we have just started an IF Function

IF=(**SUM(B4:D4)**>=100000, It is the Nested Function SUM, which means that Excel will **sum the range from B4 TO D4, therefore it will <u>sum B4, C4 and D4</u>.** It will sum 3 cells in total.

IMPORTANT NOTE: Do you realize that SUM Function also has its own parentheses? **SUM(B4:D4)** This is because to be a function (although it is inside another) it must have its same structure of **NAME(Arguments,Arguments)**

IF=(SUM(B4:D4)**>=100000,** It is the condition. We want to know if the sum of B4,C4 and D4 is greater than or equal to $100,000.

IMPORTANT NOTE: If you want to say "Greater or Equal to" the symbol of Greater To always goes before the symbol of Equal. The same applies to the Minor symbol.

Correct > =   < =

Incorrect = >   = <

Step 2: If the seller sold more than $ 100,000 the logical test will be True and the seller will earn a 2% bonus. Then the Value IF True argument should result in the bonus of 2% of the total sale.

SUM(B4:D4)*.02,

Why? Because the sum of B4: D4 (sales) will be made and 2% will be obtained.

IMPORTANT NOTE: Note that this is ANOTHER Nested Function. In this IF Function you have added 2 Nested Functions.

The formula looks like this now, but it still needs to be completed:

IF=(SUM(B4:D4)>=100000,SUM(B4:D4)* .02,

Step 3: If the seller did not sell more than $ 100,000 the logical test will be False and will not earn any bonus. Then the Value IF False argument should result in the phrase "NO BONUS".

"NO BONUS")

The COMPLETE formula looks like this:

IF=(SUM(B4:D4)>=100000,SUM(B4:D4)* .02,"NO BONUS")

And you could read like this: *"If the sum of B4, C4 and D4 is equal to or greater than $100,000 then calculate 2% of the sales and show me how much it is, if it is NOT more than $100,000 then show "No BONUS"*

	A	B	C	D	E
3	**NAME**	**JAN**	**FEB**	**MAR**	**BONUS**
4	Lavenia Ebner	$33,910	$32,316	$12,897	NO BONUS
5	Janel Joplin	$25,120	$36,424	$15,649	NO BONUS
6	KEVIN Daubert	$40,038	$48,748	$35,829	$ 2,492
7	Myles Probst	$45,911	$37,213	$24,530	$ 2,153

Now you can see which sellers got bonuses and how much.

NOTE: Another function that is similar to =SUM is =AVERAGE. It can also be used as Nested Function.

CONGRATULATIONS! Now you know how to create IF Functions with arithmetic operations and Nested Functions!

In the next chapter you will learn how to increase the number of possible outcomes. Normally you have 2 possible outcomes (Argument 2 or 3), but you will learn to add 3 or more outcomes in an endless chain of IF

Functions! It will be an interesting chapter.

SIMILAR EXERCISES:

It's time for you to solve more exercises and practice. Once you complete them you can advance to the next IF Function chapter.

Chapter4ex2.xlsx

Chapter4ex3.xlsx

QUICK CHAPTER SUMMARY:

• You learned how to use Nested Functions in different arguments of the If function

• You learned to use Sum Function as a logical test and you can also use Average in the same way.

CHAPTER 5

IF FUNCTION WITH A NESTED IF FUNCTION

This chapter is the turning point between those who are advanced users of the IF Function and those who are just beginning, so I invite you to make a lot of effort with the exercises.

You will learn to place an IF Function within another If Function within another IF Function, thus creating a larger chain that adapts the formula to solve the specific need you have.

The main advantage of creating Nested IF Functions within other IF Functions is that now the number of possible results is 3, 4, 5 or more (whichever you want, depending on how many Functions you want to nest).

I also warn you that there are several details that you will have to pay attention to and experience on your part, but those details I will highlight them as "Important Notes" so that they do not go unnoticed.

It's much easier for you to learn with an example, so let's solve an exercise.

EXERCISE: Chapter5Ex1.xlsx

You have a group of sellers, last month they sold different quantities and we need to define them in the form of TEXT without BAD, GOOD or GREAT. The requirements are the following

• **BAD: less than $ 50,000.** (When it says "less than" it means from $0 to $49,999.99, since the $50,000 would go into the next category)

• **GOOD equal to or greater than $ 50,000.** (This ranges from $50,000 to infinity, for now)

- **GREAT** Greater than $ 100,000 (This is from $100,000.01 to infinity, and this restriction requires that "GOOD" only be from $50,000 to $100,000)

IMPORTANT NOTE: Observe carefully that it is different when it says "equal or greater than" to say only "greater than".

- *"Equal or greater than $ 50,000" it also involves $ 50,000*

- *"Greater than $ 100,000" does NOT involve $ 100,000, just from 1 Cent higher, from $ 100,000.01 and above.*

NAME	SALES
Roger Vanderpool	$ 27,128
Deneen Irvine	$ 130,705
Aline Winter	$ 50,000
Marvin Tegeler	$ 87,249
Juan Samuels	$ 100,000
Niesha Hane	$ 158,159
Angela Yunker	$ 109,329
Erik Vos	$ 122,876
Ezequiel Olsson	$ 108,037

Step 1: Position yourself in cell C4 to write the formula

IMPORTANT NOTE: ALWAYS ALWAYS ALWAYS start writing the part of the formula that DOES NOT HAVE AN ESTABLISHED LIMIT. Let's explain it.

• BAD has an established limit of $0 to $49,999.99

• GOOD has an established limit from $50,000 to $100,000

• GREAT starts from $100,000.01 and DOES NOT HAVE A LIMIT

• Therefore the formula must start with the GREAT logical test

The formula starts like this:
=IF(B4>100000,"GREAT",

At this time we have the first part of the formula (the Logical test and the Value If True) that can be read like this: **"If B4 is greater than $ 100,000 then write GREAT ..."**

Step 2: Now add the 3rd argument that is Value IF False. In the 3rd argument we will add the NESTED IF FUNCTION!

=IF(B4>100000,"GREAT",IF(B4>=50000 ,"GOOD","BAD"))

In that formula there are many important things to observe:

• The Value IF False argument of the first IF Function contains another IF Function COMPLETE with its 3 arguments as well.

• In other words, the 3rd argument contains 3 other arguments.

• The end of the form has two closing parentheses, because one closes the Nested IF Function and the other closes the first IF Function.

• The last requirement (BAD) does not require any logical test, since any result that does not coincide with the previous two logical tests will result in a BAD. That is why it is important to create the formula correctly.

• **Excel processes the formula from LEFT to RIGHT. Then he reads it in the following way:**

"If B4 is greater than $ 100,000 then write GREAT ...

If it is not, then perform OTHER IF Function and ask if B4 is equal to or greater than $ 50,000, if it is then write GOOD ...

If it is not, then write BAD for any other result".

When you drag down the formula you can see the fruit of your effort.

NAME	SALES	DESCRIPTION
Roger Vanderpool	$ 27,128	BAD
Deneen Irvine	$ 130,705	GREAT
Aline Winter	$ 50,000	GOOD
Marvin Tegeler	$ 87,249	GOOD
Juan Samuels	$ 100,000	GOOD
Niesha Hane	$ 158,159	GREAT
Angela Yunker	$ 109,329	GREAT
Erik Vos	$ 122,876	GREAT
Ezequiel Olsson	$ 108,037	GREAT

Important observations:

• Aline Winter sold $ 50,000 and has a "GOOD". Remember that the formula categorized as "GOOD" the results "equal or greater than $ 50,000".

• Juan Samuels sold $ 100,000 and got a "GOOD". Remember that the formula categorized as "GREAT" only values "greater than $ 100,000", excluding values equal to $ 100,000.

CAN I NEST MORE THAN ONE IF FUNCTION AT THE SAME TIME?

The answer is, of course! Let's practice with a similar example. Open the Exercise **Chapter5Ex2.xlsx**

The sales ranges are:

• Less than $20,000 are BAD

• Equal or greater than $20,000 are FAIR

• Equal to or greater than $50,000 are GOOD

• Equal to or greater than $70,000 are GREAT

Step 1: Position yourself in cell C4 and start writing the logical test and argument 2 of GREAT.

=IF(B4>=70000,"GREAT",

Step 2: Start nesting the IF Function with the logical test for GOOD.

=IF(B4>=70000,"GREAT",IF(B4>=5000 0,"GOOD",

Step 3: Start nesting the IF Function with the logical test for FAIR and ending the formula with BAD.

=IF(B4>=70000,"GREAT",IF(B4>=5000 0,"GOOD",IF(B4>=20000,"FAIR","BAD ")))

You can read the formula this way:

• If B4 is equal to or greater than $ 70,000, write GREAT

• If not, perform another logical test: If B4 is equal to or greater than $ 50,000 write GOOD

• If not, perform another logical test: If B4 is equal to or greater than $ 20,000, write FAIR

• If not, type BAD for any other result

CONGRATULATIONS! Now you know how to nest IF Functions in a chain. Now you can get 5, 10, 15 or more different results if you nest the functions.

In the next chapter we will see a easier alternative to what you learned in this chapter. In such a way that you have both tools at your disposal.

SIMILAR EXERCISES:

It's time for you to solve more exercises and practice. Once you complete them you can advance to the next IF Function chapter.

Chapter5ex3.xlsx

QUICK CHAPTER SUMMARY:

- The Nested IF Function takes the place of the 3rd Argument and also contains its own 3 Arguments

- Excel has a limit of 64 Nested IF functions
- The next chapter will be easier than this one.

CHAPTER 6

IFS FUNCTION (EASIER ALTERNATIVE TO NESTED IF FUNCTION)

In this chapter you will learn another function, the IFS Function. It is the alternative for when you do not want to use Nested IF Functions.

The IFS Function allows you to perform many logical tests and establish a different result in case these logical tests are True.

The structure of the IFS Function is as follows:

=IFS(logical test 1,value if true 1, logical text 2, value if true 2)

• If logical test 1 is True, the formula returns the value if true 1.

• If logical test 1 is false but logical test 2 is True, it writes the value if true 2.

• If the logical tests 1 and 2 are false but the logical test 3 is True, the formula returns the value if true 3.

• And so on.

But be careful because the IFS Function does NOT have a Value IF False argument, so any value that DOES NOT match any of your logical tests will show an Error # N / A.

We will use exercises similar to those of the previous chapter so you can understand the use of IFS Function.

EXERCISE: Chapter6Ex1.xlsx

There is a group of sellers and you must categorize the sales as BAD, GOOD and GREAT:

• Sales under $ 50,000 are BAD

• Between $ 50,000 and 100,000 are GOOD

• Above $ 100,000 are GREAT

NOTE: As in the previous chapter, I recommend starting with the requirement that has NO limit, which is GREAT.

Step 1: The first thing we will do is to add 1 logical test and 1 value if true, so that you can observe what happens with the values that are not within the logical test. Position yourself in C4, write the following formula and drag it for all sales.

=IFS(B4>100000,"GREAT")

You can see that Roger gets a "GREAT" but some sellers get a # N/A. Why? Because the IFS Function does not have Value IF False, therefore the values that do not coincide with the logical tests (in this case those under $ 100,000) are not being considered in the formula.

NAME	SALES	DESCRIPTION
Roger Vanderpool	$ 127,128	GREAT
Deneen Irvine	$ 74,019	#N/A
Aline Winter	$ 36,920	#N/A

Step 2: Add the GOOD requirement to the formula, adding arguments 3 and 4

=IFS(B4>100000,"GREAT",B4>50000,"GOOD")

You can read this formula like this: **"If B4 is greater than $100,000, write GREAT, but if it is only greater than $50,000, write GOOD.**

You can see that now some sellers already have a "GOOD" instead of a #N/A

NAME	SALES	DESCRIPTION
Roger Vanderpool	$ 127,128	GREAT
Deneen Irvine	$ 74,019	GOOD
Aline Winter	$ 36,920	#N/A

SUPER IMPORTANT NOTE: IFS Function reads from LEFT TO RIGHT and returns the FIRST VALUE that matches. In other words, if both logical tests are TRUE, the value that Excel will return will be the one to the left of the formula.

Let's take the example of changing the order of the previous formula. Put the GOOD on the left and the GREAT on the right:

=IFS(B4>50000,"GOOD",B4>100000,"GREAT")

What will happen in this case is that any value above $50,000 (for example $ 200,000) will be marked with "GOOD" and not with "GREAT".

Why? Because $ 200,000 is True in the first logical test, Excel writes the Value If True 1 and does not even bother to reason the second logical test. Try it and you'll see that Roger Vanderpool gets a "GOOD" when he really deserves a "GREAT".

Step 3: Complete the formula in the correct order by adding the BAD and arguments 5 and 6.

=IFS(B4>100000,"GREAT",B4>50000,"GOOD",B4>=0,"BAD"**)**

NAME	SALES	DESCRIPTION
Roger Vanderpool	$ 127,128	GREAT
Deneen Irvine	$ 74,019	GOOD
Aline Winter	$ 36,920	BAD
Marvin Tegeler	$ 87,249	GOOD
Juan Samuels	$ 134,023	GREAT
Niesha Hane	$ 158,159	GREAT
Angela Yunker	$ 95,023	GOOD
Erik Vos	$ 43,918	BAD
Ezequiel Olsson	$ 108,037	GREAT

CONGRATULATIONS! Now you know how to use the **IFS Function**. It's much simpler than using the **Nested IF Functions, but you need to know both methods.**

SIMILAR EXERCISES:

It's time for you to solve more exercises and practice. Once you complete them you can advance to the next IF Function chapter.

Chapter6ex2.xlsx

Chapter6ex3.xlsx

QUICK CHAPTER SUMMARY:

- IFS Function can replace the use of Nested IF Functions
- IFS Function has no Value If False
- If no logical test is true you get #N/A
- If all the logical tests are true you get the Value If False that is first in the formula.

CHAPTER 7

IF FUNCTION WITH A NESTED "OR" FUNCTION

OR Function is a way to add more complexity and depth to your formula. It is very simple to use and understand.

In short, the OR Function nested within the logical test of the IF Function allows you to add several logical tests. It only takes one of all those logical tests to be true for the IF Function to consider the whole formula as True

Let's do an exercise to explain it step by step.

EXERCISE: Chapter7Ex1.xlsx

In this exercise, you are supposed to be a

salesperson trying to decide which product is best for you to sell. You have a list of products that include the commission percentage, the time required to sell the product and the sale price.

To make the analysis you have 3 criteria, and you have decided that if 1 of the 3 criteria is met, the product is worth to sell it. The 3 criteria are the following:

• That the commission is greater than 25%

• That the product requires less than 5 hours of effort to sell it

• That the product is sold for more than $ 1500

Step 1: Position yourself in E4 and start writing the formula, nesting OR in the logical test of IF

$$=IF(OR($$

After that it is necessary that you write the 3 logical tests. In other words, the OR

Function will take the place of the logical IF test, thus allowing to create several logical tests instead of one.

=IF(OR(logical test1,logical test 2,logical test3),

The formula for now would look like this:

=IF(OR(B4>.25,C4<5,D4>1500),

Step 2: Add the Value IF True and Value If False of the IF Function and drag the formula for all products

=IF(OR(B4>.25,C4<5,D4>1500),"OK"," Not OK")

NAME	% Comision	Hours to Sell	Sale Price	To Sell or Not?
Product 1	20%	2	$ 1,300	OK
Product 2	30%	5	$ 2,100	OK
Product 3	40%	4	$ 1,950	OK
Product 4	25%	8	$ 3,000	OK
Product 5	15%	1	$ 1,500	OK

Why did everyone get "OK"? Because all products meet at least 1 of the 3 established requirements.

This is how the OR Function works. If 1 requirement is fulfilled, IF Function will consider the whole formula True

Cool! Now you know how to use the OR Function nested in the IF Function.

SIMILAR EXERCISES:

It's time for you to solve more exercises and practice. Once you complete them you can advance to the next IF Function chapter.

Chapter7ex2.xlsx

Chapter7ex3.xlsx

QUICK CHAPTER SUMMARY:

- The nested OR Function takes the place of the logical IF Function test

- The OR Function allows you to create several logical tests
- If any of the logical tests of OR is True, the IF Function considers the formula to be True

CHAPTER 8

IF FUNCTION WITH A NESTED "AND" FUNCTION

In this chapter you will learn how to nest the AND Function within the IF Function. The good news is that the procedure is exactly the same as with the OR Function.

The Nested AND Function serves to create several logical tests (like OR) but the big difference is that ALL the logical tests must be True so that the IF Function considers that the formula is true. If a logical AND test is False (although all others are true), the IF Function will consider the formula false.

Let's do an exercise to explain it step by step.

EXERCISE: Chapter8Ex1.xlsx

We will use an exercise similar to the one in the last chapter, so you can observe the similarities and differences between OR and AND.

In this exercise, you are supposed to be a salesperson trying to decide which product is best for you to sell. You have a list of products that include the commission percentage, the time required to sell the product and the sale price.

To make the analysis you have 3 criteria, and you have decided that you need ALL the criteria to be met to decide that it is a good product to sell. The 3 criteria are the following:

• That the commission is greater than 25%

• That the product requires less than 5 hours of effort to sell it

• That the product is sold for more than $ 1500

Step 1: Position yourself in E4 and start writing the formula, nesting AND in the logical test of IF

=IF(AND(

After that, it is necessary that you write the 3 logical tests. In other words, the AND Function will take the place of the logical IF test, thus allowing to create several logical tests instead of one.

=IF(AND(logical test1,logical test 2,logical test3),

The formula for now would look like this:

=IF(AND(B4>.25,C4<5,D4>1500),

Step 2: Add the Value IF True and Value If False of the IF Function and drag the formula for all products

=IF(AND(B4>.25,C4<5,D4>1500),"OK", "NO")

NAME	% Comision	Hours to Sell	Sale Price	To Sell or Not?
Product 1	20%	2	$ 1,300	NO
Product 2	30%	5	$ 2,100	NO
Product 3	40%	4	$ 1,950	OK
Product 4	25%	8	$ 3,000	NO
Product 5	15%	1	$ 1,500	NO

You can observe that only Product 3 is good enough to invest your time in selling it, since it is the one that has the most potential for profit taking into account the 3 criteria mentioned above.

This is how the AND Function works. It is necessary that ALL the criteria are True so that the IF Function considers the formula True.

CONGRATULATIONS! Now you know how to use the AND Function nested in the IF Function.

SIMILAR EXERCISES:

It's time for you to solve more exercises

and practice. Once you complete them you can advance to the next IF Function chapter.

Chapter8ex2.xlsx

Chapter8ex3.xlsx

QUICK CHAPTER SUMMARY:

• The AND Function is used in the same way as OR

• It is necessary that ALL the logical tests of the AND Function are True to get the Value If True.

CHAPTER 9

SUMIF AND SUMIFS FUNCTIONS

You have completed your training of the functions that are directly related to the IF Function. The first 8 chapters were dedicated to teach you the following:

• The IF Function

• IF Function within another IF Function

• IFS Function

• OR Function within an IF Function

• AND Function within an IF Function

Now you need to learn to use 4 more formulas:

• SUMIF

- SUMIFS

- COUNTIF

- COUNTIFS

You will learn the first 2 in this chapter and the last in the next chapter.

The SUMIF Function is used to sum the cells that meet one criterion. Meanwhile, the SUMIFS Function is used to sum the cells that meet 2 or more criteria.

In other words, the SUMIFS Function is stricter than the SUMIF Function.

Now you will learn to use the 2 with the same exercise.

EXERCISE: Chapter9Ex1.xlsx

You have a sales list of 3 Products, country of sale and color of the product. You must make 3 different calculations:

1. Revenue of Product 1 (With SUMIF)

2. Revenue of Product 1 sold to USA (with SUMIFS)

3. Revenue of Product 1 sold to USA in RED color (with SUMIFS)

	A	B	C	D	E	F	G	H	I
3	PRODUCT	COUNTRY	COLOR	REVENUE					
4	Product 1	USA	BLUE	$ 456,837		CALCULATE THE SALES WITH THIS CRITERIA			
5	Product 2	USA	YELLOW	$ 891,119					
6	Product 3	GERMANY	RED	$ 399,654		Product 1			
7	Product 2	ENGLAND	BLACK	$ 684,141		Product 1	USA		
8	Product 3	GERMANY	WHITE	$ 422,908		Product 1	USA	RED	

The structure of the SUMIF formula is the following:

=SUMIF(range,criteria,sum range)

How do you read that? If the "criteria" is in the "range", then Excel sums the value found in the "sum range" in the same row where the "criteria" was found.

RANGE: It is the range (group of cells) where you will look for the Criterion you want. In the exercise the Range would be A4:A18. Why? Because there are the names of the Products that were sold.

CRITERIA: It is the requirement that you are looking for. In the exercise it is "Product 1" or F6.

SUM RANGE: It is where the values to be added are found. In the exercise it is D4:D18 since there is the Revenue.

Step 1: Position yourself in Cell I6, write the following formula.

=SUMIF(A4:A18,F6,D4:D18)

Now you can see that the Revenue of Product 1 is **$2,100,105.** How was that amount obtained? Look at the following image.

| SUMA | ▲▼ | ✕ ✓ | *fx* | =SUMIF(A4:A18,F6,D4:D18) |

	A	B	C	D	E	F	G	H
3	**PRODUCT**	**COUNTRY**	**COLOR**	**REVENUE**				
4	Product 1	USA	BLU	$ 456,837		**CALCULATE THE SALES WIT**		
5	Product 2	USA	YELLOW	$ 891,119				
6	Product 3	GERMANY	RED	$ 399,654		Product 1		
7	Product 2	ENGLAND	BLACK	$ 684,141		Product 1	USA	
8	Product 3	GERMANY	WHITE	$ 422,908		Product 1	USA	RED
9	Product 1	CANADA	RED	$ 426,983				
10	Product 2	ENGLAND	BLACK	$ 279,944				
11	Product 2	GERMANY	WHITE	$ 101,631				
12	Product 3	CANADA	YELLOW	$ 553,440				
13	Product 2	USA	RED	$ 919,687				
14	Product 3	GERMANY	BLACK	$ 209,387				
15	Product 1	USA	WHI	$ 806,606				
16	Product 3	CANADA	RED	$ 189,183				
17	Product 3	ENGLAND	BLUE	$ 354,904				
18	Product 1	GERMANY	BLU	$ 409,679				

• Excel found the "criteria" that is F6 or "Product 1" within Range A4: A18, found it 4 times, in rows 4, 9, 15 and 18

• After that the formula added the values in the Sum Range (column D) of the same rows 4, 9, 15 and 18.

Now you know how to use SUMIF! It is very simple. In the next steps we will use SUMIFS.

The structure of the SUMIFS formula is as

follows:

$$=\text{SUMIFS}(\textbf{sum range},\text{criteria range1,criteria1,criteria range 2, criteria 2})$$

SUM RANGE: It is where the values to be added are found. In the exercise it is D4:D18 since there is the Revenue.

CRITERIA RANGE 1: It is the range (group of cells) where you will look for the FIRST Criterion you want. In the exercise the Range would be A4:A18 Why? Because there are the names of the Products that were sold.

CRITERIA 1: FIRST is the requirement you are looking for. In the exercise it is "Product 1" or F7.

CRITERIA RANGE 2: It is the range (group of cells) where you will look for the SECOND Criterion you want. In the exercise the Range would be B4 B18 Why? Because there are the names of the Countries

CRITERIA 2: It is the SECOND requirement that you are looking for. In the exercise it is "USA" or G7.

Step 2: In cell I7 we will use the following formula

=SUMIFS(D4:D18,A4:A18,F7,B4:B18,G7)

Now you can see that only 2 sales meet both criteria.

	A	B	C	D	E	F	G	H
	SUMA		fx	=SUMIFS(D4:D18,A4:A18,F7,B4:B18,G7)				
3	PRODUCT	COUNTRY	COLOR	REVENUE				
4	Product 1	USA	BLUE	$ 456,837		CALCULATE THE SALES WIT		
5	Product 2	USA	YELLOW	$ 891,119				
6	Product 3	GERMANY	RED	$ 399,654		Product 1		
7	Product 2	ENGLAND	BLACK	$ 684,141		Product 1	USA	
8	Product 3	GERMANY	WHITE	$ 422,908		Product 1	USA	RED
9	Product 1	CANADA	RED	$ 426,983				
10	Product 2	ENGLAND	BLACK	$ 279,944				
11	Product 2	GERMANY	WHITE	$ 101,631				
12	Product 3	CANADA	YELLOW	$ 553,440				
13	Product 2	USA	RED	$ 919,687				
14	Product 3	GERMANY	BLACK	$ 209,387				
15	Product 1	USA	WHITE	$ 806,606				
16	Product 3	CANADA	RED	$ 189,183				
17	Product 3	ENGLAND	BLUE	$ 354,904				
18	Product 1	GERMANY	BLUE	$ 409,679				

Step 3: Finally, in cell I8 we will use the

following formula

=SUMIFS(**D4:D18**,A4:A18,F8,B4:B18,G8,C
4:C18,H8)

You can observe in your exercise that NO sale meets all 3 criteria at the same time.

CONGRATULATIONS! Now you know how to use SUMIF and SUMIFS.

In the next chapter you will learn how to use COUNTIF and COUNTIFS, which are very similar to the formulas you learned in this chapter

SIMILAR EXERCISES:

It's time for you to solve more exercises and practice. Once you complete them you can advance to the next IF Function chapter.

Chapter9ex2.xlsx

QUICK CHAPTER SUMMARY:

• SUMIF is a formula that requires 1 criterion to be met.

• SUMIFS requires 2 or more criteria

• Both are very similar to each other.

CHAPTER 10

COUNTIF AND COUNTIFS FUNCTIONS

It's time for you to learn how to use COUNTIF and COUNTIFS. Both are very similar to the functions of the previous chapter.

The COUNTIF Function is used to COUNT the times that 1 criterion is met. Meanwhile, COUNTIFS Function is used to COUNT the times that 2 or more criteria are met.

In other words, the COUNTIFS Function is stricter than the COUNTIF Function.

Now you will learn to use the 2 with the same exercise.

EXERCISE: Chapter10Ex1.xlsx

You have a sales list of 3 Products, country of sale and color of the product. You must count the times that the following criteria are met:

1. Product 1 (With COUNTIF)

2. Product 1 sold to USA (with COUNTIFS)

3. Product 1 sold to USA in RED color (with COUNTIFS)

	A	B	C	D	E	F	G	H	I
3	PRODUCT	COUNTRY	COLOR	REVENUE					
4	Product 1	USA	BLUE	$ 456,837		HOW MANY TIMES IS THIS CRITERIA MET?			
5	Product 2	USA	YELLOW	$ 891,119					
6	Product 3	GERMANY	RED	$ 399,654		Product 1			
7	Product 2	ENGLAND	BLACK	$ 684,141		Product 1	USA		
8	Product 3	GERMANY	WHITE	$ 422,908		Product 1	USA	RED	

The structure of the COUNTIF formula is as follows:

=COUNTIF(range,criteria)

How do you read it? If the "criteria" is in the "range", then Excel COUNTS how many times the "criteria" is found in that "range".

RANGE: It is the range (group of cells) where you will look for the Criterion you want. In the exercise the Range would be A4:A18 Why? Because there are the names of the Products that were sold.

CRITERIA: It is the requirement that you are looking for. In the exercise it is "Product 1" or F6.

Step 1: Position yourself in Cell I6, write the following formula.

=COUNTIF(A4:A18,F6)

Now you can see that Product 1 was sold 4 times. How was that number obtained?

• Excel found the "criteria" that is F6 or "Product 1" within Range A4:A18, found it 4 times, in rows 4, 9, 15 and 18

Now you know how to use

COUNTIF! It is very simple. In the next steps we will use COUNTIFS.

The structure of the COUNTIFS formula is as follows:

=SUMIFS(criteria range1,criteria1,criteria range 2, criteria 2)

CRITERIA RANGE 1: It is the range (group of cells) where you will look for the FIRST Criterion you want. In the exercise the Range would be A4:A18 Why? Because there are the names of the Products that were sold.

CRITERIA 1: FIRST is the requirement you are looking for. In the exercise it is "Product 1" or F7.

CRITERIA RANGE 2: It is the range (group of cells) where you will look for the SECOND Criterion you want. In the exercise the Range would be B4:B18 Why? Because there are the names of the Countries

CRITERIA 2: It is the SECOND requirement that you are looking for. In the exercise it is "USA" or G7.

Step 2: In cell I7 we will use the following formula

=COUNTIFS(**A4:A18,F7,B4:B18,G7**)

Now you can see that only 2 sales meet both criteria.

PRODUCT	COUNTRY	COLOR	REVENUE
Product 1	USA	BLUE	$ 456,837
Product 2	USA	YELLOW	$ 891,119
Product 3	GERMANY	RED	$ 399,654
Product 2	ENGLAND	BLACK	$ 684,141
Product 3	GERMANY	WHITE	$ 422,908
Product 1	CANADA	RED	$ 426,983
Product 2	ENGLAND	BLACK	$ 279,944
Product 2	GERMANY	WHITE	$ 101,631
Product 3	CANADA	YELLOW	$ 553,440
Product 2	USA	RED	$ 919,687
Product 3	GERMANY	BLACK	$ 209,387
Product 1	USA	WHITE	$ 806,606
Product 3	CANADA	RED	$ 189,183
Product 3	ENGLAND	BLUE	$ 354,904
Product 1	GERMANY	BLUE	$ 409,679

Step 3: Finally, in cell I8 we will use the following formula

=COUNTIFS(A4:A18,F8,B4:B18,G8,C4:C18,H8)

You can observe in your exercise that NO sale meets all 3 criteria at the same time.

CONGRATULATIONS! Now you know how to use COUNTIF and COUNTIFS.

SIMILAR EXERCISES:

It's time for you to solve more exercises and practice. Once you complete them you can advance to the next IF Function chapter.

Chapter10ex2.xlsx

QUICK CHAPTER SUMMARY:

• COUNTIF is a formula that requires 1

criterion to be met.

• COUNTIFS requires 2 or more criteria

• Both are very similar to each other and serve to count the number of times that one or more criteria appear within a data table.

CONGRATULATIONS!

If you have completed the chapters and the exercises, you are now an IF Function Champion!

Because of your effort, I decided to share with you the first chapter of my previous books:

- **EXCEL PIVOT TABLE CHAMPION**
- **EXCEL VLOOKUP CHAMPION**
- **EXCEL CONDITIONAL FORMATTING CHAMPION**

Also, in the last chapter I have included several tips that I consider important for your development as an Excel Champion.

CHAPTER 11

BONUS CHAPTER:
EXCEL PICOT TABLE CHAMPION
FRAGMENT

WHAT IS A PIVOT TABLE AND WHICH ARE ITS BENEFITS?

__As a Bonus and Free Gift, you are getting the 1st Chapter of my book "Excel Pivot Table Champion".__

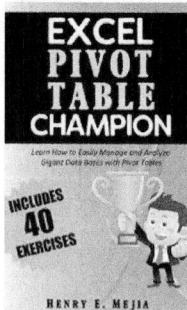

A Pivot Table is absolutely one of the best tools in Excel, the benefits of knowing how to use this tool are a lot since in most cases it is almost impossible to manually perform the work done by the Pivot Table tool.

If you want to do the work manually you would spend at least 10 times more time, it is better to invest that time learning to use the Pivot Tables.

"By using a Pivot Table the right way, you can get the answers you want in 10% of the time (or less)"

A Pivot Table is used to manage giant data tables (which we will call Source Data from now on), so you can organize the information and get the relevant answers you want.

A Source data can have thousands and thousands of rows of information and dozens of columns. To show an example, let's say that a table contains the following columns of information:

- Order ID
- Date
- Region

- Sales Agent
- Item
- Units sold
- Cort Per Unit
- Revenue per unit
- Profit per unit
- Total Cost
- Total Revenue
- Total Profit
- Express Shipping

That would be 13 columns, if the table had 1,000 Order IDs, you would have a Source Data with 13,000 individual cells.

If you are asked the following questions, what would you answer?

• Which agent sold more refrigerators in the North zone?

• How much profits have TVs generated with express delivery and without express delivery?

• What percentage of revenue does the West zone have in relation to total revenue?

Probably you tend to use filters and some formulas to answer these questions, losing your most valuable asset, your time. But if you know how to use the Pivot Tables, you can answer that in less than a minute (Literally in less than a minute when you're already a Pivot Table Champion)

Let's answer the first question from the previous example. **Which agent sold more refrigerators in the North zone?**

First, this is how the Source Data would be.

Note: (The Source Data with which we are going to practice throughout this book has 500 rows of information and 13 columns, 6500 data in total)

ORDER ID	DATE	REGION	SALES AGENT	ITEM	UNITS	COST PER UNIT	REVENUE PER UNIT	PROFIT PER UNIT	TOTAL COST	TOTAL REVENUE	TOTAL PROFIT	EXPRESS SHIPPING
1231	12/03/18	West	Viki Jerabek	Refrige	11	$300	$450	$150	$3,300	$4,950	$1,650	YES
1232	13/03/18	North	Sana Ulery	TV	55	$200	$300	$100	$11,000	$16,500	$5,500	NO
1233	14/03/18	East	Leida Schow	Kitchei	48	$350	$500	$150	$16,800	$24,000	$7,200	YES
1234	15/03/18	South	Christiane Polen	Home	43	$150	$300	$150	$6,450	$12,900	$6,450	NO
1235	16/03/18	North	Tonja Berk	Air Cor	43	$250	$500	$250	$10,750	$21,500	$10,750	NO
1236	17/03/18	East	Rolando Blanc	TV	65	$200	$300	$100	$13,000	$19,500	$6,500	YES
1237	18/03/18	South	Casandra Mullaney	Kitchei	78	$350	$500	$150	$27,300	$39,000	$11,700	NO
1238	19/03/18	West	Erik Vos	Home	46	$150	$300	$150	$6,900	$13,800	$6,900	YES
1239	20/03/18	North	Ezequiel Olsson	Refrige	91	$300	$450	$150	$27,300	$40,950	$13,650	NO
1240	21/03/18	North	Selena Haddad	TV	78	$200	$300	$100	$15,600	$23,400	$7,800	NO

This would be the answer with a Pivot Table (which took less than 1 minute). **Cassandra, Christiane and Ezequiel sold more Refrigerators, tied with 4 each in the North zone.**

ITEM Count	East	North	South	West	TOTAL
▼ Casandra Mullaney	1	4	1	1	7
Refrigerator	1	4	1	1	7
▼ Christiane Polen		4		1	5
Refrigerator		4		1	5
▼ Erik Vos	3		1		4
Refrigerator	3		1		4
▼ Ezequiel Olsson	1	4	1		6
Refrigerator	1	4	1		6
▼ Rolando Blanc	3	2	2	1	8
Refrigerator	3	2	2	1	8
▼ Sana Ulery		2	1		3
Refrigerator		2	1		3
▼ Selena Haddad	1	2	4	1	8
Refrigerator	1	2	4	1	8
▼ Tonja Berk	2	1		1	4
Refrigerator	2	1		1	4
▼ Viki Jerabek		1		1	2
Refrigerator		1		1	2
TOTAL	11	20	10	6	47

It may sound ironic, but the Pivot Table is probably the most useful tool and one of the easiest to use once you learn a few tricks.

The benefits of learning to use Pivot Tables are the following:

• You save a huge amount of time. The larger the Source Data, the more time you save, since you do not have to do calculations manually.

• You can create organized Tables just like you want to show the information, so in your work meetings you can perfectly communicate your insights

• You can combine it with the Conditional Formatting tool (see my Excel Conditional Formatting Champion book for more information)

• You can use charts that reflect the information of your Pivot Table

• You have access to answers and insights that you could not get in any other way.

QUICK CHAPTER SUMMARY:

• The Pivot Table is probably the tool that can save you more time and effort

• Answer almost all the questions you can ask about a Database (Source Data)

• You can get very good findings using Pivot Tables with your company information

• They are very simple to use once you have learned and practiced

CHAPTER 12

BONUS CHAPTER:
VLOOKUP CHAMPION FRAGMENT

WHAT IS VLOOKUP AND WHICH ARE ITS BENEFITS?

As a Bonus and Free Gift, you are getting the 1st Chapter of my book "Excel Vlookup Champion".

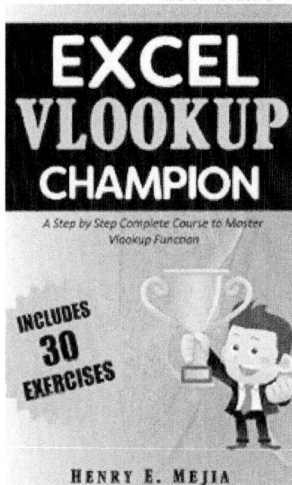

WHAT IS A FUNCTION?

An Excel function is a tool used to make calculations, searches, changes or logical reasoning with data you provide, with the objective of returning a result.

Functions (or formulas) always start with the symbol of =

Every time you try to write a function you must select the cell and start with a =

In a simple way, using functions saves you the hard work and it is Excel who works hard to give you the result you are looking for. Less work for you and less time in the office!

"Using functions (formulas) saves you a lot of hard work."

Excel is one of the most powerful software, it has many functions and many tools, and in this book you will learn one of the most useful: VLOOKUP

WHAT IS VLOOKUP?

Vlookup is one of the most useful Excel functions. You can use it in different ways but **basically it helps you find information within a giant amount of data.**

IMPORTANT NOTE:

VLOOKUP is the formula in English.

If you use Excel in Spanish, the formula works the same, with the only difference that VLOOKUP in Spanish is called BUSCARV.

You only need to enter in the formula = BUSCARV instead of = VLOOKUP and voila, everything else remains the same.

Sometimes, you need to find the exact price (or any other information) of a certain Product ID, but you have many products. What someone who is not a Vlookup Champion does is to search the price of each product in their database and copy it manually, one by one. What a waste of time! What a Vlookup Champion does is to use the formula to get the right prices from the database and in 30 seconds all the prices along with their respective Product ID are in place, with zero errors.

If you have a list of names or numbers and you need to relate it to other data, Vlookup helps you find that

information in a database, in just a few seconds and without errors

It is possible that you have a list of students, clients, stores, employees, vehicles, invoices, and you need to place certain information next to them without errors to be able to do an analysis with or without graphs, VLOOKUP helps you to do that in a matter of seconds.

EXAMPLE:

Imagine that you have this daily sales table, and you need to fill out the product description and the employee who sold it:

PRODUCT ID	EMPLOYEE ID	PRODUCT DESCRIPTION	EMPLOYEE NAME
4	111		
5	110		
1	110		
3	113		
1	112		
1	111		
2	111		

It would take you easily 3 or 4 minutes to fill it out manually and with the risk of having errors, and there are only 7 sales. When you face hundreds of sales you can end up with some complications. But if you have previously a "master table" where you have the list of all the product IDs and their descriptions **(that "master table" is called Database** and it is usually obtained from the ERP System of the business) you can use Vlookup and within 15 seconds you will have the product descriptions in order. Another 15 seconds and you would have the names of the employees too.

When you are a Vlookup Champion you need only 1 minute to search and write

what used to take you 10 minutes without Vlookup

THE BENEFITS OF USING VLOOKUP AS A CHAMPION

Well, it's obvious that knowing how to use Vlookup doesn't make you look sexier in the office (although sometimes it does) but it has many other benefits:

• You can save a lot of time of searching and filling spreadsheets with information of databases. That is, you have more chances to leave the office early and have done what they ask.

• Most of the time you will have zero errors, and when you have one you can immediately notice it. Never again give incorrect information to the boss. Avoid ending up the day with a long face.

• Vlookup makes it easy for you to learn

other Excel functions. Combining functions is one way to get the best out of Excel, and using Vlookup as a Champion is a great start to achieve that.

• You can spend more time analyzing the information and searching ways to improve your work. How on earth can you analyze the information if you use hours to obtain it and organize it? By the time you finish you are tired, stressed and hungry! It's better to use VLOOKUP.

Now that you understand the benefits of being a Vlookup Champion, you will be more motivated to be one. In the next chapter you will learn the parts that make up the Vlookup function quickly and easily. Once you understand the structure and its parts you will begin with the exercises.

QUICK CHAPTER SUMMARY

- Vlookup will save you time and prevent you from making mistakes.
- Vlookup will allow you to analyze more information and make better decisions in your job or business.

CHAPTER 13

BONUS CHAPTER:
EXCEL CONDITIONAL
FORMATTING CHAMPION
FRAGMENT

As a Bonus and Free Gift, you are getting the 1st Chapter of my book "Excel Conditional Formatting Champion".

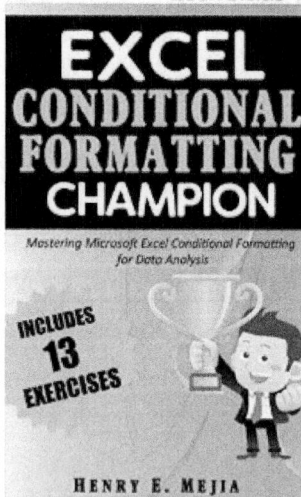

WHAT IS CONDITIONAL FORMATTING AND WHICH ARE ITS BENEFITS?

In Excel, "formatting" means visually changing a cell. Some examples of format are:

• Center the words
• To align to the right
• Fill the cell with one color
• Underline the words
• Words in bold
• Modify the font color
• Modify the size of the words

Conditionals in Excel are logical sequences that normally follow the pattern "If the CONDITION is met, then Excel FORMATS the cell". Some types of conditions are:

• The value of the cell is lower or higher than other
• The value of one cell is the same as another
• The cell contains a certain letter, word or phrase

- The values are duplicated within a group of several cells
- The values are within a range of dates
- The values are the minimum or maximum values within a group of cells
- Many other conditions can be added

So, to explain it simply, CONDITIONAL FORMAT means to automatically format a cell (with any of the previous formatting options) when the condition we want is fulfilled.

"CONDITIONAL FORMAT means to automatically format a cell when the condition we want is met"

With the conditional formatting tool, it is extremely easy to automatically highlight the information that interests you, allowing you to recognize important information for decision making in a matter of seconds.

CONDITIONAL FORMATTING EXAMPLES

EXAMPLE 1: Imagine for a moment

that you need to find 10% of the higher values in the following table.

$ 12,987	$ 10,013	$ 15,374	$ 17,859	$ 15,357
$ 21,063	$ 21,960	$ 24,124	$ 16,694	$ 20,379
$ 24,548	$ 27,985	$ 18,331	$ 20,087	$ 20,738
$ 16,338	$ 12,128	$ 14,737	$ 29,622	$ 22,304
$ 13,077	$ 18,284	$ 17,242	$ 25,142	$ 21,184
$ 26,904	$ 22,268	$ 29,995	$ 23,040	$ 14,467
$ 10,899	$ 11,486	$ 17,632	$ 18,182	$ 14,930
$ 24,807	$ 23,216	$ 10,814	$ 23,004	$ 28,096
$ 13,543	$ 22,207	$ 25,858	$ 16,111	$ 17,892
$ 28,782	$ 14,308	$ 17,011	$ 26,171	$ 13,980
$ 19,498	$ 24,938	$ 21,053	$ 24,735	$ 20,536
$ 15,145	$ 20,030	$ 29,021	$ 20,080	$ 11,518
$ 23,545	$ 26,763	$ 25,402	$ 10,900	$ 21,565

The conditional formatting tool helps you achieve it easily in less than 20 seconds. When you order Excel to find 10% of the higher values and color the cell in green automatically.

In this example, the condition was "10% of the top group values". The group consists of 65 values, 10% is 6.5, so Excel automatically formatted the 6 cells that are the higher.

$	12,987	$	10,013	$	15,374	$	17,859	$	15,357
$	21,063	$	21,960	$	24,124	$	16,694	$	20,379
$	24,548	$	27,985	$	18,331	$	20,087	$	20,738
$	16,338	$	12,128	$	14,737	$	29,622	$	22,304
$	13,077	$	18,284	$	17,242	$	25,142	$	21,184
$	26,904	$	22,268	$	29,995	$	23,040	$	14,467
$	10,899	$	11,486	$	17,632	$	18,182	$	14,930
$	24,807	$	23,216	$	10,814	$	23,004	$	28,096
$	13,543	$	22,207	$	25,858	$	16,111	$	17,892
$	28,782	$	14,308	$	17,011	$	26,171	$	13,980
$	19,498	$	24,938	$	21,053	$	24,735	$	20,536
$	15,145	$	20,030	$	29,021	$	20,080	$	11,518
$	23,545	$	26,763	$	25,402	$	10,900	$	21,565

EXAMPLE 2: Now we have a table with sales, names and brands of mobile phones. You want to find the 20 smallest values.

As I mentioned, with conditional format it is extremely easy to highlight information you need. In the image below, you can see that in a matter of seconds you found the 20 smallest values.

	SAMSUNG	NOKIA	LG	SONY	MOTOROLA
Sana	$ 25,182	$15,106	$14,214	$21,754	$ 22,467
Leida	$ 16,480	$22,342	$11,612	$16,884	$ 18,968
Christiane	$ 29,702	$16,465	$13,584	$21,947	$ 25,785
Tonja	$ 13,228	$16,234	$13,451	$13,646	$ 28,438
Rolando	$ 16,312	$16,925	$27,171	$29,930	$ 17,889
Casandra	$ 17,862	$21,929	$16,906	$24,335	$ 27,516
Erik	$ 25,135	$27,831	$17,250	$23,910	$ 24,126
Ezequiel	$ 10,219	$13,363	$18,215	$16,910	$ 25,343
Selena	$ 27,335	$25,834	$23,222	$21,479	$ 20,898
Milly	$ 11,262	$18,933	$19,868	$15,405	$ 12,259
Herminia	$ 20,576	$23,796	$20,746	$22,146	$ 15,732
Juan	$ 15,396	$16,610	$16,251	$13,622	$ 17,499
Niesha	$ 27,445	$18,241	$14,086	$20,714	$ 20,854

The relevant information that you can obtain in this simple example is that:

• Tonja is the one with the most difficulty to sell almost all the brands.
• The brand that sells more easily is Motorola.

That information is very valuable to make decisions. In this simple example you can realize that conditional format is eally useful , now imagine the benefit you can get when you use that same tool for more complex situations.

EXAMPLE 3: Now you have a similar table with the profits per company and you want to know the best ones, the average ones and the worst ones. Also you want to know which year was the best, and you want the information in a simple and visual way.

	A	B	C	D	
2011	$26,554	$49,876	$11,209	$32,464	$ 120,103
2012	$44,826	$17,609	$38,542	$46,752	$ 147,729
2013	$41,809	$34,980	$35,947	$18,187	$ 130,923
2014	$13,194	$48,279	$28,524	$23,020	$ 113,017
2015	$39,276	$29,444	$21,095	$44,220	$ 134,035
2016	$20,459	$41,733	$35,966	$46,671	$ 144,829
2017	$18,803	$28,459	$47,940	$16,684	$ 111,886

Notice that in a matter of seconds you can color the values in a degraded way, the one with the darkest color is the highest value, the one with no color is the lowest value, and all the intermediate ones are shown with a color scale .

Additionally to the right is the sum of all of the sales of each year, which includes a bar visually indicating the information in the form of a graph. Those two things can also be done with conditional formatting.

The number of situations in which conditional formatting can be used are a lot and it usually offers a quick and visually comfortable solution to analyze and present information.

QUICK CHAPTER SUMMARY:

• The Conditional Formatting tool is used to format a cell automatically.

• Formatting means changing the shape, color, size or background of a cell or group of cells.

• Conditional format offers a quick and visually comfortable solution to analyze and present information.

CHAPTER 14

QUICK FINAL EXCEL TIPS

This book wouldn't be complete without a series of final recommendations that can help you to be not only an If Function Champion, but also a complete Excel Champion.

Here (in this short chapter) I can't teach you everything I'm going to recommend because they are extensive topics that would not fit in a few pages, it is also information that I teach deeply in other Excel Champions books.

However, I want to make you the following recommendations with the hope that you recognize the main tools that you must learn to be an Excel Champion.

WHY DO YOU NEED TO LEARN TO USE PIVOT TABLES?

The Excel Pivot Tables tool is one of the most powerful and effective in Excel. They serve to summarize information from giant databases and you can get a lot of information that you would not otherwise be able to.

You can learn everything you need about Pivot Tables in my Excel Pivot Table Champion book.

WHY DO YOU NEED TO LEARN KEYBOARD SHORTCUTS?

First of all, I want to recommend that you learn Excel keyboard shortcuts. Keyboard shortcuts are the easiest and fastest way to increase your productivity in Excel. You can easily cut your work time in half.

The reality is that there are more than

100 keyboard shortcuts. My recommendation is that you learn the 10 or 20 main ones. Which are the main ones? The ones you use the most depending the kind of work you have to do in Excel.

Some of those that everybody should use are:

Ctrl + C to copy a cell (with format too)

Ctrl + V to paste the cell that you copied

Ctrl + X to cut the cell (instead of copying it, you remove it from its cell to paste it in another cell)

Ctrl + to insert a column or row (selecting the column or row previously)

Ctrl - to delete a column or row (selecting the column or row previously)

Surely with these shortcuts you can move a little faster. But there are more that are quite useful.

WHY DO YOU NEED TO LEARN

VLOOKUP?

The VLOOKUP formula is one of the most used FOR search and reference in Excel.

When you work with large amounts of data (numeric and text) it is very likely that you have to use the formulas VLOOKUP, IF, MATCH or INDEX.

Every one of these formulas are explained in my Excel Vlookup Champion book

WHY DO YOU NEED TO LEARN MORE FUNCTIONS?

There are hundreds of functions that can help you to better perform your work, however, you may not know them. Sometimes a new function that you learn can save you hours of weekly work in the office.

The important fact to remember about functions is that they tend to relate to each other and become stronger tools when combined or in the form of nested formulas.

I'll give you an example: VLOOKUP. The VLOOKUP function is quite strong and useful on its own, but when you learn to use IF together with VLOOKUP, three things happen:

1) You learned a new function: VLOOKUP

2) You learned a new function: IF

3) You learned a new tool: IF + VLOOKUP

When you learn just two functions you actually have three tools in your toolbox. That is, your tools are not just the number of functions you master, but also include the combinations you can make between those functions.

So the more functions you know, the more combinations you can make and the more chances you have to become an Excel Champion.

I WOULD LOVE TO READ YOUR COMMENTS

Before you go, I would like to tell you Thank You for buying my book. I hope that the information you obtained in Excel IF FUNCTION Champion helps you in your job or business, and that you can have greater productivity and more free time to use it in the activities that you like the most.

I realize that you could have chosen among several other Excel books but you chose Excel IF FUNCTION Champion and you invested your time and effort. I am honored to have the opportunity to help you.

I'd like to ask you a small favor. **Could you take a minute or two and leave a Review of Excel IF FUNCTION Champion on Amazon?**

This feedback will be very appreciated and will help me continue to write more courses that help you and a lot more people.

Share your comments with me and other readers.

ABOUT THE AUTHOR

Henry E. Mejia is an online entrepreneur who discovered the great benefits of knowing how to use Microsoft Excel at an advanced level, and now he devotes part of his time to creating courses (books and videos) so that more people can enjoy free time and better opportunities that an Advanced Excel user can have.

Henry also realized that the vast majority of people give away a lot of their life in front of the computer. That time could be used in more productive or more enjoyable activities, only if people knew how to use Excel a little better.

The goal of Henry's books is to open the door for workers and business owners to use Excel more efficiently, so they can have more and better growth opportunities.

Printed in Great Britain
by Amazon

86521803R00071